CONTENTS

Copyright ©2020 ARNOLD KUNTZ PH.D

INTRODUCTION

Summer perfection is the crisp taste of tender zucchini, lightly steamed and dipped in olive oil, or even better the soft folds of the Cucurbita pepo blooms, stuffed with equally velvety flavours such as goat's cheese, salmon or lemon. Whether you are growing your own or selecting from a well-stocked greengrocer, these are the true fruits of summer abundance. Zucchini is the Italian name, meaning gourd, and encompasses the whole group of squash, marrows, pumpkins and other similar growing cucurbits. The French coined the term courgettes d'Italie, and the English borrowed that for their description. In America they are known as summer squash, after the season in which they are best grown. Whatever the name, the fruit is at its best very young and immature. If left on the plant, it quickly becomes a marrow. The flowers are interesting all by themselves. Very delicate, the large orange blooms open and expand in one day   hopefully enough time to attract a bee to spread the pollen from the male flower to the female. The male flower forms beside leaves on the plant's main stem and is often prized for canapés and starters in Italian cuisine, due to its long stem. Female flowers are found on the growing fruit, and can be eaten in a more raw state.

HISTORY

Zucchini was originated in Mexico where it has been domesticated for at least 5,000 years. It extended to Northern Mexico and Southwestern U.S. During the 16th century, it got introduced to Europe. In Italy, it is considered to be occurred in late nineteenth century. China, Japan, Italy, Romania, Turkey, Italy, Argentina and Egypt are known as the biggest producers of squash. It is cultivated all year round and consumed raw in a sliced form.

PLANT

Zucchini is an annual vine that has shallow, branched and well developed taproots. The leaves are alternate, simple, large, broadly triangular and dark green. The fruit of Zucchini is white, pale-dark green-yellow having a variable shapes and 1 meter long. The fruit bears flattened seeds of obovoid- elliptic shape and white to pale brown in color. The stem is hard, angular, five-angled, semi-erect and pubescent to scabrous. The plant bears bright yellow flowers that are pentamerous and solitary.

NUTRITIONAL VALUE

One cup of 113 grams of raw Zucchini contains 18 calories, 1.37 grams of protein, 0.2 grams of lipid fat, 1.2 grams of dietary fiber and 2.49 grams of total sugars. The same amount offers about 21.33% of Vitamin C, 18.92% of Vitamin B6 and 12.31% of Vitamin B2.

ZUCCHINI FACTS

Zucchini, also known as courgette is a type of summer squash that belongs to the pumpkin family. Summer squash is part of human diet starting from 5.500 years BC. It originates from Central and South America. Summer squash was introduced to Europe in the 16th century. Type of summer squash known as zucchini was created during the 19th century in Italy. Zucchini grows in warm, dry climate, on well-drained, moist soil. It represents one of the most popular and most commonly consumed vegetable today. China is the greatest manufacturer of squashes in the world.

Interesting Zucchini Facts:

Zucchini is bushy plant. It has light green, prickly stem that can reach 2.93 feet in height.

Zucchini develops large, lobed, green leaves covered with silver-gray blotches on the surface.

Zucchini blooms early in the summer. It produces individual male and female flowers on the same plant (monoecious). Male flowers are slightly smaller. They grow from the axils of leaves. Female flowers develop on top of the branches. Flowers are yellow colored and they attract bees, responsible for the pollination.

Fruit of zucchini is sausage-shaped pepo (berry with thick skin on the surface). Color of the fruit varies from light to dark green, depending on the cultivar. Flesh is creamy white, juicy, soft and filled with numerous tiny, edible seed. Largest ever recorded zucchini had 69.5 inches in length and 65 pounds of weight.

Hybrid known as golden zucchini produces yellow or orange-colored fruit.

Zucchini is usually harvested 8 weeks after fertilization of the female flowers, when it reaches the length of 8 inches. Fruit needs to be harvested before it reaches full maturity, while it is still tender on the outside and filled with soft, edible seed on the inside. Zucchini is an excellent source of dietary fibers, vitamins A, C and B9 (folate) and minerals such as manganese and potassium. Zucchini contains 93% of water and only 23 calories.

Dark-colored zucchini contains the greatest amount of nutrients. Small and medium-sized zucchini have better flavor than large varieties. Compound called cucurbitacin accumulates in the fruit when plant grows exposed to high temperature in areas that do not provide enough water and nutrients in the soil. As a result, fruit has bitter taste.

Zucchini can be consumed raw, but they are usually thermally processed before consumption. They can be used for the preparation of salads, casseroles and breads.

Both male and female zucchini flowers are edible. They can be fried, stuffed and baked.

Zucchini are also used in the cosmetic industry for the manufacture of various soaps.

Word "zucchini" originates from Italian word "zucca" which means "squash".

Nutrients from the zucchini have potential to prevent development of cancer and cardiovascular disorders.

Zucchini is an annual plant which means that it completes its life cycle in one year.

One zucchini is a "zucchina."

Zucchinis were first brought to the United States in the 1920s by the Italians.

April 25th is National Zucchini Bread Day.

The flower of the zucchini plant is edible. Fried squash blossoms are considered a delicacy.

Mild bitterness in zucchini, like that in related species like cucumbers, may be result from environmental factors such as high temperature, low moisture, low soil nutrients, etc. The bitterness is caused by compounds called cucurbitacins.

The world's largest zucchini on record was 69 1/2 inches long, and weighed 65 lbs. Bernard Lavery of Plymouth Devon, UK, grew it.

Nutrients and vitamins found in zucchini can help prevent cancer and heart disease.

A zucchini has more potassium than a banana.

The word zucchini comes from 'zucca' the Italian word for squash.

Biggest is NOT best. The most flavorful zucchinis are small-to medium-sized and the darker the skin, the richer the nutrients.

ZUCCHINI NUTRITION INFORMATION

(per 1 large (323g) zucchini, raw, with skin) Note: Leave the skin on the zucchini! It contains a bulk of the nutrients, especially Vitamin A, Vitamin K, and fiber.

Calories: 52

Carbohydrates: 11g

Fiber: 4g, 14% Daily Value (DV)

Protein: 4g

Fat: 1g

92% DV of Vitamin C: A water-soluble vitamin that acts as an antioxidant to fight against potentially damaging free radicals (molecules with unshared electrons that float around wreaking havoc) and an important cofactor in collagen synthesis.

35% DV of Vitamin B6 (Pyridoxine): A water-soluble vitamin that works behind the scenes as a coenzyme in many important reactions within your body, including protein metabolism and red blood cell formation, among countless other functions.

28% DV of Manganese: A trace element that plays a role in healthy brain and nervous system function.

27% DV of Riboflavin (Vitamin B2): A water-soluble vitamin that acts as a component of FAD to help your body break down macronutrients in the electron transport chain, creating usable energy.

24% DV of Potassium: A key mineral and electrolyte involved in countless processes, including healthy nervous system functioning and contraction of the heart and muscles.

23% DV of Folate (Vitamin B9): A water-soluble vitamin that helps make DNA & RNA and metabolize amino acids.

17% DV of Vitamin K: A fat-soluble vitamin that allows for activation of enzymes in the clotting cascade, which is responsible for blood clotting. Also builds bone by modifying osteocalcin so that it may bind calcium, thus building the bone matrix.

13% DV of Vitamin A: Provides the provitamin version of this fat-soluble vitamin, meaning it comes from a plant source and your body converts the plant pigment into active Vitamin A. It is essential in many components of healthy vision, as well as immunity and cell growth/differentiation.

10% DV of Thiamin (Vitamin B1): A water-soluble vitamin that turns your food (carbohydrates) into fuel (glucose). People at risk for deficiency include those with Crohn's Disease, alcoholics, and those undergoing kidney dialysis.

Zucchini is a summer squash, much like pumpkins and eggplant. Zucchini are similar to cucumbers in appearance, but have a very different texture. They range from light green to very dark green (almost black) in color and can even have stripes. Zucchini can grow to be over a foot, but are harvested at different sizes around the world. In the United States, zucchini is typically harvested when it is between 5 and 8 inches long (approximately 2 to 7 days after flowering), but in South Africa the fruit is harvested when it is still very small (about the size of your finger) and is called 'baby marrows'.

SEASONALITY

Squash is separated into two categories: summer squash and winter squash. Summer squash has a high water content and thin edible skin. Zucchini is the most popular of summer squashes and is "in season" from May until August, but can be found in the grocery store all year long. Smaller, younger zucchini have more flavor, so pick one that is firm with a glossy, unblemished skin. You can store your zucchini for up to five days in the refrigerator.

FRUIT OR VEGETABLE?

Although zucchini is typically treated as a vegetable, when it comes to culinary situations, it is technically a fruit. The zucchini itself is actually the swollen ovary of the zucchini flower. Zucchini was first introduced in the Americas, but the zucchini that we know and love today was developed in Italy many generations after they were originally introduced. Unlike many other fruits, zucchini does not have a large amount of natural sugar, but it does have a high water content and is low in calories. It is also a good source of folic acid, potassium, and vitamins A and C.

VARIETY

Just like every other fruit, there are many varieties of zucchini ranging in color, size, length of time to produce and texture. White squash, or summer squash, is sometimes seen as a mutation of the zucchini and is even found on the same plant as its' green relatives. Originally, zucchini was only grown in its traditional long cylindrical version, but newer varieties have surfaced more recently to meet the ever growing demand of cooks near and far. Golden zucchini and globe zucchini are the newest varieties of zucchini that have been grown for commercial purposes. Golden zucchini is the same shape as traditional green zucchini, but has a lighter color and a lighter flavor. Globe zucchini, on the other hand, is green in color but is spherical, more similar to a pumpkin. These globe zucchinis are about 3 inches in diameter on average and are perfect for stuffing.

ZUCCHINI FLOWERS

Zucchini flowers are one of a select few edible flowers. The flowers, also called courgette flowers, can be eaten raw or cooked. I typically think of myself as someone who has tried plenty of exotic or out of the ordinary foods, but zucchini flowers are something I had never even thought of eating.

USES

Zucchini is a vegetable that is delicious by itself but I can also be used for a variety of meals anywhere from breakfast to dessert after dinner. Because its flavor isn't exceptionally strong, zucchini can be added or baked into traditional recipes to give it a hint of flavor and some added health benefits. Chilled zucchini soup during the summer is a refreshing way to try something new.

HOW TO COOK IT

Zucchini can be baked in the oven with other vegetables or by itself with olive oil and spices. It can also be sautéed on the stove to make a delicious vegetable side for any meal. Deep fried zucchini fritters are a delicious snack and are slightly healthier than French fries.

THE BEST SEASONINGS FOR ZUCCHINI

When you think of seasoning fruits and vegetables, typically salt and pepper come to mind instantly, but there are a few other ways to spice up your zucchini and they are even salt free. Basil and oregano go incredibly well with zucchini and so do some of our seasoning blends. Our Roasted Garlic Pepper is fantastic for garlic lovers and our Habanero Garlic Pepper is made especially for cooks who are always looking for an added kick. Any way you slice it, zucchini is a great addition to so many dishes and even great on its own with a few seasonings. The next time you see them at a roadside stand or farmers market make sure to pick up a few and try out a healthy new recipe. It might surprise you how versatile zucchini can be!

HOW TO BUY

Zucchini and its flowers should be sourced when very fresh. The fruit or the swollen cylindrical tubes are crispest on the day of picking and have a rapid respiration rate, becoming limp very easily. Look for fresh crisp fruit, with no scarring, or bruising. Because life is so short for the flowers, they are chilled and often sold with the petals closed. If the flower is too old, it will be impossible to open and stuff or even remove the stamen inside.

HOW TO STORE

These are the ultimate fresh produce. Don't even try to keep zucchini flowers for long they should be cooked and eaten on the day of picking. If they must be stored, lightly mist with water and place in a ziplock plastic bag in the fridge. Zucchini will last a few more days, but need to be wrapped in plastic, and kept in the vegetable section of the fridge. They can be frozen: simply slice and place in a bag. Use within three months.

HOW TO GROW

Zucchini are grown from seed at the earliest signs of spring, when the soil begins to warm. Keep at least half a metre between plants, as they spread. A good tip for space-saving is to plant them inside a cone cage, like ones used for training beans or tomatoes, so they grow up, not out. They will require a well-manured soil, plenty of water, in a sunny, sheltered spot. Downy mildew and sap-sucking insects are the enemy, so keep an eye on the large prickly leaves and treat swiftly.

PREPARATION TIPS

Small zucchinis are delectable raw. Slice into batons for the crudité platter, grated or sliced into salads and mixed with the best vinaigrette; included in a coleslaw; or thrown into a green smoothie.

REDUCE WASTE

Sometimes, it seems, all the zucchini are ready to be picked at once. At times of abundance, excess produce can easily be made into soups, stews, frittatas, or even bread, muffins and cakes. There is no meal where the average zucchini can't slip into. However, if the garden zucchini have grown too large, don't leave them rotting for the birds and insects. The larger of the fruit are perfect peeled and thinly-sliced used as a layer in a vegetable lasagne, or grated for soft breads, cakes, pasta, fritters, or even added to muffins and omelettes. Really large ones can be stuffed with wild rice and mince-meat for a delicious quick dinner. Even the discarded tops of the zucchini can be thinly sliced and marinated and added to a Thai green curry or salad.

THINGS YOU SHOULD KNOW ABOUT ZUCCHINI

If you want a veggie that's extremely versatile, look no further than zucchini. Whether eaten raw or cooked, there's so many ways to enjoy it and still get a solid amount of a few vitamins and minerals you need. Zucchini actually falls under the umbrella of summer squash, which are squashes that get harvested before their rinds harden (unlike, say, pumpkins and butternut squash). Here are some other fun facts about this veggie that may surprise you.

First, how many calories are in zucchini?
Not many in fact zucchini is super low in calories and makes the perfect light side dish for a heavy meal: One cup of sliced zucchini has about 19 calories. That's 40 to 50% lower than the same serving size for other low-cal green veggies like broccoli and Brussels sprouts. And because it's so versatile, you can enjoy this low-calorie food in so many different recipes, from baked fries to pesto roll-ups. Of course, you can always grill zucchini with herbs for some savory flavor, too.

You can eat the blossoms
Even though zucchini is served as a vegetable, it's tech-

nically a fruit because it comes from a flower: it grows from a golden blossom that blooms under the leaves. They don't normally sell the blooms in the grocery store, but you can find them at farmers' markets. And these beauties aren't just for looking at you can eat them, too. The most popular way to prepare them is fried or stuffed.

Zucchini may be good for your heart

Zucchini has a good amount of potassium: 295 milligrams per cup, or 8% of your recommended daily value. Potassium can help control blood pressure because it lessens the harmful effects of salt on your body. Studies suggest boosting your potassium intake (while also curbing sodium) can slash your stroke risk and may also lower your odds of developing heart disease. Zucchini is also high in the antioxidant vitamin C, which may help the lining of your blood cells function better, lowering blood pressure and protecting against clogged arteries. One cup of sliced zucchini has 20 milligrams, or about 33% of your daily value.

You can substitute it for pasta

Sure, you can add zucchini to your spaghetti recipes, but you can also use it in place of noodles altogether. So-called "zoodles" are a great pasta alternative, and they're easy to make with the help of some kitchen gadgets. With a mandolin or a spiral slicer, you secure the zucchini on prongs and push the veggie toward the blades. Not only does it make things easy, but it's also kind of cool to see dozens of noodles cranked out at once. A smaller and less expensive option is a julienne peeler, which has a serrated blade to create thin strips.

It's not always green

You may be used to seeing a vegetable that's green and speckled, but there's a yellow variety of zucchini, and it's easy to confuse with yellow squash, a different type. The easiest way to tell the difference is to look at the shape.

Yellow squash usually has a tapered neck, either crooked or straight, whereas zucchini of any color looks like a cylinder from end to end. Though not much is known about the difference between the varieties, some say golden zucchini has a sweeter flavor than the green kind. Because it retains its color after cooking, it also makes a sunny addition to any dish.

It has an international pedigree
Italians are thought to have bred modern zucchini from the squash they picked up in colonial America. "Zucca" is actually the Italian word for squash. That's why you'll see zucchini referred to as "Italian squash" in some recipes. Still, summer squash has been around for quite some time. The crop dates back to 5500 B.C. where it was integral in the diets of people living in Central America and South America, according to the University of Arizona Cooperative Extension. (And if you're in Europe, it may appear on menus as "courgette.

HEALTH AND NUTRITION BENEFITS OF ZUCCHINI

Zucchini, also known as courgette, is a summer squash in the Cucurbitaceae plant family, alongside melons, spaghetti squash, and cucumbers. It can grow to more than 3.2 feet (1 meter) in length but is usually harvested when still immature typically measuring under 8 inches (20 cm). Although zucchini is often considered a vegetable, it is botanically classified as a fruit. It occurs in several varieties, which range in color from deep yellow to dark green. While squashes originated in the Americas, this particular variety was first developed in the early 1800s in Italy. Zucchini has been used in folk medicine to treat colds, aches, and various health conditions. However, not all of its uses are backed by science.

1. Rich in Many Nutrients

Zucchini is rich in several vitamins, minerals, and other beneficial plant compounds.

One cup (223 grams) of cooked zucchini provides:

Calories: 17

Protein: 1 gram

Fat: less than 1 gram

Carbs: 3 grams

Sugar: 1 gram

Fiber: 1 gram

Vitamin A: 40% of the Reference Daily Intake (RDI)

Manganese: 16% of the RDI

Vitamin C: 14% of the RDI

Potassium: 13% of the RDI

Magnesium: 10% of the RDI

Vitamin K: 9% of the RDI

Folate: 8% of the RDI

Copper: 8% of the RDI

Phosphorus: 7% of the RDI

Vitamin B6: 7% of the RDI

Thiamine: 5% of the RDI

It also contains small amounts of iron, calcium, zinc, and several other B vitamins. In particular, its ample vitamin A content may support your vision and immune system. Raw zucchini offers a similar nutrition profile as cooked zucchini, but with less vitamin A and more vitamin C, a nutrient which tends to be reduced by cooking. Zucchini contains a variety of vitamins, minerals, and beneficial plant compounds. Cooked zucchini is particularly high in vitamin A, though raw zucchini contains slightly less.

2. High in Antioxidants

Zucchini is also rich in antioxidants. Antioxidants are beneficial plant compounds that help protect your body from damage by free radicals. Carotenoids such as lutein, zeaxanthin, and beta-carotene are particularly plentiful in zucchini. These may benefit your eyes, skin, and heart, as well as offer some protection against certain types of cancer, such as prostate cancer. Research indicates that the skin of the plant harbors the highest levels of antioxidants. Yellow zucchinis may contain slightly higher levels than light green ones. Zucchini boasts several antioxidants that may provide various health benefits. The highest levels are found in the fruit's skin.

3. Contributes to Healthy Digestion

Zucchini may promote healthy digestion in several ways. For starters, it's rich in water, which can soften stools. This makes them easier to pass and reduces your chances of constipation. Zucchini also contains both soluble and insoluble fiber.

Insoluble fiber adds bulk to stools and helps food move through your gut more easily, further reducing constipation risk. This benefit is compounded if you have enough fluids in your diet. Meanwhile, soluble fiber feeds the beneficial bacteria living in your gut. In turn, these friendly bacteria produce short-chain fatty acids (SCFAs) that nourish your gut cells. What's more, SCFAs may help reduce inflammation and symptoms of certain gut disorders, such as irritable bowel syndrome (IBS), Crohn's disease, and ulcerative colitis. Zucchini is rich in water and fiber, two compounds which can promote healthy digestion by reducing your risk of constipation and symptoms of various gut disorders.

4. May Reduce Blood Sugar Levels

Zucchini may help lower blood sugar levels in people with type 2 diabetes. At 3 grams of carbs per cooked cup (232 grams), zucchini provides a great low-carb alternative to pasta for those looking to reduce carb intake. It can be spiralized or sliced to replace spaghetti, linguini, or lasagna noodles in dishes. Low-carb diets can significantly lower blood sugar and insulin levels, both of which may keep blood sugar levels stable and reduce the need for medication in people with type. What's more, zucchini's fiber helps stabilize blood sugar, preventing levels from spiking after meals. Diets rich in fiber from fruits and vegetables including zucchini are consistently linked to a lower risk of type 2 diabetes.

The fiber found in zucchini may also help increase insulin sensitivity, which can help stabilize blood sugar as well. Additionally, animal studies note that zucchini peel extract may help reduce blood sugar and insulin levels. This may be due to the skin's potent antioxidants. However, human research is needed before strong conclusions can be made. Zucchini's fiber may increase insulin sensitivity and stabilize blood sugar levels, potentially reducing your risk of type 2 diabetes.

5. May Improve Heart Health

Zucchini may also contribute to heart health. Its high fiber content may be largely responsible. Observational studies show that people who eat more fiber have a lower risk of heart disease.

Pectin, one type of soluble fiber found in zucchini, appears particularly effective at reducing total and "bad" LDL cholesterol levels. In a review of 67 studies, consuming as little as 2–10 grams of soluble fiber per day for around

1–2 months reduced, on average, total cholesterol by 1.7 mg/dl and "bad" LDL cholesterol by 2.2 mg/dl. Zucchini is also rich in potassium, which may help reduce high blood pressure by dilating your blood vessels. Healthier blood pressure is linked to a lower risk of heart disease and stroke. Moreover, diets rich in carotenoids likewise found in zucchini appear particularly protective against heart disease. The fiber, potassium, and carotenoids in zucchini may lower blood pressure, cholesterol, and other risk factors for heart disease.

6. May Strengthen Your Vision

Adding zucchini to your diet may aid your vision. That's partly because zucchini is rich in vitamin C and beta-carotene two nutrients important for eye health. Zucchini also contains the antioxidants lutein and zeaxanthin. Research shows that these antioxidants can accumulate in your retina, improving your vision and reducing your risk of age-related eye diseases. This may include a lower risk of macular degeneration, which is the leading cause of irreversible vision loss in older adults in addition, diets high in lutein and zeaxanthin may also lower your likelihood of developing cataracts, a clouding of the lens which can lead to poor eyesight. Zucchini is rich in manganese, lutein, zeaxanthin, and vitamins A and C nutrients which contribute to healthy vision and may lower your risk of age-related eye conditions.

7. May Aid Weight Loss

Regular consumption of zucchini may help you lose weight. This fruit is rich in water and has a low calorie density, which may help you feel full. Its fiber content may also reduce hunger and keep your appetite at bay. Moreover, studies consistently link high fruit and vegetable intake to weight loss and a slower rate of weight gain over time. What's more, intake of non-starchy, dark green or yellow vegetables with similar nutrition profiles to zucchini appears particularly beneficial to weight loss. Zucchini is rich in water and fiber yet low in calories, all of which may help reduce hunger and help you feel full potentially leading to weight loss over time.

8. Other Potential Benefits

Zucchini may offer some additional benefits. The well-researched include:

Bone health. Zucchini is rich in the antioxidants lutein and zeaxanthin, as well as vitamin K and magnesium, all of which can help strengthen bones.

Anticancer effects. Test-tube and animal studies indicate that zucchini extracts may help kill or limit the growth of certain cancer cells. However, human research is needed.

A healthy prostate. Animal research shows that zucchini seed extracts may help limit prostatic hyperplasia, an enlargement of the prostate that commonly causes urinary and sexual difficulties in older men.

Thyroid function. Testing in rats reveals that zucchini peel extracts may help keep thyroid hormone levels stable. That said, research in humans is needed.

Zucchini may benefit bone, thyroid, and prostate health. It may also have anticancer properties. However, more research is needed before strong conclusions can be made.

9. Easy to Add to Your Diet

Zucchini is incredibly versatile and can be eaten raw or cooked. Here are some ways to incorporate it into your meals:

Add it raw to salads.

Stew it with other summer fruits and vegetables to make ratatouille.

Stuff with rice, lentils, or other vegetables, then bake it.

For a mild stir-fry, add olive oil and sauté it.

Boil it, then blend it into soups.

Serve it as a side, grilled or sautéed with a little garlic and oil.

Try it breaded and fried.

Spiralize it into spaghetti- or linguine-like noodles, or slice it to replace lasagna sheets.

Bake it into breads, pancakes, muffins, or cakes.

HEALTH BENEFITS OF ZUCCHINI

Though Zucchini is a fruit, it is treated as vegetable. The skin, flesh and seeds of Zucchini are edible. It offers a great taste when it is cooked. It possesses light and sweet taste. The minerals, nutrients and vitamins found in Zucchini helps to maintain heart health, eye health, reduce cholesterol, strengthen bones and teeth as well as promote weight loss.

Assist in weight loss
Zucchini has low amount of calories but also it helps to keep full. It satisfies the stomach without more calories and is a healthy diet plan. Zucchini has high amount of water and fiber along with the low amount of calories. Those people who are on diet should add Zucchini which provides enormous health benefits.

Maintains overall health
Zucchini is an excellent source of Vitamin C and Manganese which helps to maintain the health. Magnesium, Vitamin A, Copper, Potassium and Phosphorus are also contained in Zucchini. Additionally, it has high amount of zinc, protein, niacin, omega 3 fatty acids, Vitamin B6, Vitamin B1, Vitamin B2 as well as calcium. The pregnant women should consume Zucchini due to the high amount of fiber.

Enhance men health

The research has shown that the properties found in Zucchini helps to cure BPH (Benign Prostatic Hypertrophy). Due to the enlargement of prostate gland, there will be difficulty in the urinary and sexual function which is called prostatic hypertrophy. Zucchini helps to treat the BPH symptoms if combined with the foods that are rich in phytonutrients.

Prevent diseases

The regular consumption of Zucchini helps to prevent diseases and various health ailments. The studies have shown that the foods rich in fiber help to relieve cancer by clearing out the toxins from the colon cells. Zucchini contains folate, Vitamin C and beta carotene which protect the cells from the chemicals that lead to colon cancer. Vitamin C and Beta-carotene possess anti-inflammatory properties which help to cure the ailments such as asthma, osteoarthritis, swelling and rheumatoid arthritis.

Cardiovascular health

Zucchini has high amount of Vitamin C and Manganese which is required to maintain the healthy heart. It prevents atherosclerosis and heart disease. Beta-carotene helps to prevent the cholesterol oxidation. The vitamin folate helps to eliminate homocysteine levels that lead to strokes and heart attacks. The fiber content in Zucchini reduces the level of cholesterol which also decreases the chances of heart disease, atherosclerosis caused due to diabetes.

Prevent stroke

The study shows that the high amount of Vitamin C in the blood helps to lower the chances of stroke by 42%. The people who consume veggies and fruits have high level of

Vitamin C in the blood so one should increase the intake of veggies and fruits to prevent the chances of stroke.

Brain health

Vitamin B6 helps in the development of brain and its function. The deficiency of Vitamin B6 results in low memory, cognitive impairment, dementia and Alzheimer's. Vitamin B6 impact on the brain function by controlling the level of homocysteine that leads to heart ailments and damage the neurons of central nervous system.

Vitamin B6 is vital for the norepinephrine and serotonin which controls the energy, mood and concentration. The research shows that ADHD on children is the cause of low level of serotonin. Vitamin B6 may help the children on recovering the behavior and learning disorders.

Enhance mood

Vitamin B6 has great impact on the GABA neurotransmitters and serotonin in brain which helps to control mood, prevent pain, depression, anxiety and fatigue. Vitamin B6 helps to prevent mood disorders and enhance mood. Vitamin B6 helps to produce hormones in the brain which helps to treat brain diseases and mood disorders. The research shows that the supplements of Vitamin B6 uplift the mood, concentration, energy and experience less pain.

Treat migraines

Vitamin B2 helps to treat migraine headaches effectively. Riboflavin of 400 mg dose helps to treat the headaches and cure the migraine attacks. The riboflavin supplements acts as a natural aid to lower the migraine frequency, lower the symptoms, pain caused by migraine and also minimizes the duration.

Antioxidant activity

Vitamin B2 is an antioxidant which restricts the existence of free radicals in the body. It is essential for the glutathione production which detoxifies the liver and body. Vitamin B2 defends the body from the diseases by managing the healthy lining in the digestive tract where immune system is stored. The digestive system assists in the nutrient absorption. The deficiency of riboflavin leads to the less utilization of nutrients for the energy.

Riboflavin helps to prevent cancers such as esophageal cancer, colorectal cancer, prostate cancer and cervical cancer. Though more study should be carried out to find out the role of Riboflavin in the prevention of cancer. But it is considered that Vitamin B2 helps to lower the effects of oxidative stress and carcinogens which are caused due to the free radicals.

TRADITIONAL USES

The seed can prevent the kidney stones.

In Africa, pulp is used as poultice to cure burns, inflammations and as a cooling compress as a treatment for neuralgia and headache.

It is also applied to corns and tumors.

Seeds are consumed as an anthelmintic.

In Mauritius, seeds infusion is used internally for treating prostate complaints and hypertension whereas the external use helps in treating erysipelas.

HOW TO EAT

The immature fruits are consumed as vegetables by steamed, grill, boiled, baked, stuffed, fried, hollowed or barbequed. In West Africa, the fruits are added to soups, stews and couscous.

Zucchini are used in the preparation of various cuisines.

Zucchini is added to salads in Mexico.

In Italy, Zucchini is breaded or pan fried.

In Libya, Zucchini is filled with rice, minced meat, herbs, and spices and then steamed.

In Bulgaria, fried Zucchini are served with dip which is made from garlic, yoghurt and dill.

The flowers are deep fried, stuffed, baked, sautéed or added in soups.

The seeds are consumed raw, roasted or as snacks.

Flowers are stuffed, battered or deep fried to make a Japanese dish called tempura.

Courgette farcie is a French dish which is prepared by filling bell papers or tomatoes in Zucchini.

Turkey dish named mücver is a pancake made from zucchini, flour, eggs which is gently fried in olive oil and consumed with yogurt.

The mashed Zucchini could be served as a side dish.

OTHER FACTS

Italians brought Zucchinis to the United States in 1920s.

April 25th is celebrated as National Zucchini Bread Day.

Mild bitterness in Zucchini may be a result of low moisture, high temperature, low soil nutrients, etc.

The world's largest zucchini on record weighed about 65 lbs and was 69 1/2 inches in length.

The vitamins and nutrients found in zucchini help to prevent heart disease and cancer.

Zucchini contains more potassium in comparison to banana.

TYPES OF ZUCCHINI

There are various types of Zucchini which possess a distinct characteristics which from others. Every Zucchinis are not dark green and round. Few widespread types are listed here with explanations:

1. Spineless Beauty Zucchini

Spineless Beauty Zucchini is desirable to those with hyper-sensitive skin which gets annoyed through the spines of Zucchinis plants. The foliage and stems are without spines and bears fruit prolifically. It is 8 inch long, smooth, deep green and possess a rich taste.

2. Aristocrat Zucchini

Aristocrat this variety has a wax like skin and moderate green. Aristocrat Hybrid yields Zucchini during an entire season. The fruits are slim, dark green and up to 7-8" in length. The waxy skin consists of white flesh inside.

3. Black beauty Zucchini

Black beauty Zucchini It has dark green skin with creamy white flesh. It is added to salads, soups and casseroles. It could be sliced thin to dips, fried, battered or as vegetable lasagna.

4. Zucchini Gadzukes

Zucchini Gadzukes It is exclusive dark green which have light green ridges. When the slices are made it seems star-shaped. It possess sweet flavor and is crispy. It does well in full sun and common soil.

5. Gold Rush Zucchini
Gold Rush Zucchini is a variety of genus Cucurbita pepo var. cylindrical. It is a hybrid variety. Gold Rush Zucchini has a vibrant, wax like golden to yellow skin that protects the creamy flesh. It is an annual plant which grows up to the height of 90 cm (2.93 feet). It is plant which requires low maintenance.

6. Greyzini Zucchini
Greyzini Zucchini has creamy grey to green fruits which is fairly sweet, delicious and has rich taste. It is an annual plant which grows up to 90 cm (2.93 feet) high. It blossoms at the beginning of the summer.

7. Sweet Gourmet Zucchini
Zucchini Sweet gourmet is an annual plant which grows upto 90 cm or 2.93 feet high. The plant blooms at the beginning of the summer.

8. Zucchini 'Dark Green'
Zucchini 'Dark Green'It is a hybrid variety with dark green fruits which are mottled with pale green flesh. It possess a fragile flavor. It has the lifecycle of one year. It grows up to 90 cm high.

9. Zucchini 'Burpee's Fordhook'
Zucchini 'Burpee's Fordhook has smooth, round, deep blackish to green and curved fruits. The flesh is creamy white and sensitive. It also grows upto the height of 90.0 cm. It blossoms during early summer.

10. Zucchini 'Cocozelle'
Leaves of this variety are Kelly green in color. It is a tiny bush which produce dark green Zucchinis with light green

stripes. It is effective for canning and freezing. It has the life cycle of one year. It grows up to 90.0 cm high. This particular variety has a tendency to bloom during the early summer.

11. Zucchini 'Black Jack'

Zucchini 'Black Jack'Black Jack possess a dark green fruit which is about 15 cm (6 inch) long. The fruit is lengthy, dark green with creamy to white flesh. It is an annual plant which grows up to 90 cm (2.93 feet) high.

12.'Golden Zucchini'

'Golden Zucchini' Leaves are rough and India green in color. The immature fruit is 20 to 30 cm long. Golden Zucchini grows to the height of 90 cm or 2.93 feet. It is considered to be arrived from Italy.

13. Zucchini 'Ronde de nice'

Zucchini 'Ronde de nice'The leaves of Ronde de nice are cadmium green and pale silver in color. Zucchini of French heirloom produces tiny, light green spherical Zucchini. Italian heirloom are spherical, green, possess soft & fine flavor. Deep green leaves possess the silver veins. Ronde de nice is an annual plant which grows up to 90 cm or 2.93 feet high. This variety is derived from France.

14. Zucchini 'Defender'

Zucchini 'Defender 'It is grown an annual plant which grows up to 90 cm or 2.93 feet high. This variety blooms at a beginning of the summer. Defender is raised from Italy.

15. Baby Zucchini

The flesh of Baby Zucchini is firm and seedless. They could be pickled along and cooked with other techniques. It doesn't need long time to cook and may be steamed or blanched.

16. Green Zucchini

Green zucchini has smooth, deep green, shiny skin and has one inch long green stem. This variety is versatile as it can be prepared in several ways such as roasted, steamed, grilled, baked, fried and boiled.

17. Yellow Zucchini

The yellow courgettes has the similar taste of green courgettes. It has vibrant yellow skin and strong flesh with green stems.

18. Italian Zucchini

Italian zucchini is cooked similarly as standard zucchinis. This variety is green, lengthy and thin. They are cultivated in Italy.

HOW TO COOK ZUCCHINI

Zucchini is made up of 95% water, so while cooking water will drip out. It could be added to bread recipe as well. The daily intake of Zucchini helps to balance the overall health for a long term.

10 ways to cook zucchini
1. Grilled Zucchini Parmesan
Thicker slices of the grilled Zucchini should be layered with a basil leaves, warm tomato sauce and grated Parmesan in order to have a meatless main course.

2. Zucchini Carpaccio
Slice Zucchini in a thin way. Take 1/4 cup of white wine vinegar, one crumb of honey and sprinkle of salt and pepper. Stir in 1/4 cup of olive oil. Then drizzle zucchini with adequate vinaigrette for a light coat. Stand for about fifteen minutes before serving. Top with asiago cheese. Then serve at a room temperature.

3. Crisp Zucchini Gratin
Zucchini should be sliced in a lengthy strips. Then layer in a baking dish and spread salt and pepper. Scatter with breadcrumbs and asiago or parmesan. Roast it until Zucchini is soft and the breadcrumbs are light golden. It requires about twenty- thirty minutes. Serve it hot.

4. Zucchini Crostini

Steam thick Zucchini rounds till it becomes soft. Sprinkle pinches of salt and newly ground pepper. Each round should be topped with a small dollop of light ricotta. After the nutmeg is sprinkled serve it Immediately.

5. Zucchini Noodles

Peel long and thin strips of Zucchini with the use of a veggie peeler. Cook it in boiling water until it is soft for about one to two minutes. Toss with a pasta sauce and vegetables.

6. Zucchini Shrimp Stir-Fry

Put a vegetable oil in a fry pan or wok. Add quartered baby bok choy and strips of Zucchini. Stir fry it till it is soft. Add chopped garlic with a squeezed lime juice. Then add shrimp and stir fry it till shrimp becomes pink and vegetables becomes soft. Serve it over the cooked buckwheat soba noodles. Season it with hot chili garlic sauce, garlic, sesame oil and lime juice.

7. Zucchini Quinoa Salad

Cook quinoa by following the package directions. Steam chunks of Zucchini and broccoli florets by spreading it over quinoa for a couple of minutes. When the quinoa is completed, allow it to become cool. Stir it in a pinches of cayenne pepper, dollop of Dijon mustard and squeeze in a lemon juice. Stir to coat and serve along with main course.

8. Grilled Zucchini Ratatouille

Grill the ratatouille vegetables such as zucchini, tomatoes, eggplant and peppers. When it becomes cool chop it coarsely. Toss with an extra virgin olive oil, fresh lemon juice, pepper, sliced fresh oregano and salt. Add navy beans or top with cheese. Served it warm or at room temperature.

9. Zucchini Slaw

Slice zucchini in thin or bite size strips. Mix the light mayo with fresh lemon juice and a pinch of salt. Drizzle mayo mixture over the Zucchini strips to gently coat. Stir it to combine. Then serve it instantly.

10. Edamame, Zucchini and Chicken Salad

Boiling edamame by following the package directions. Add chunks of Zucchini with edamame only at the last minutes of cooking. Drain it properly. Cool it a little bit, then toss with the chunks of cooked breast of chicken and baby greens such as arugula or spinach. Top with a low fat dressing.

THINGS YOU DIDN'T KNOW ABOUT ZUCCHINI

When it comes to summer produce, zucchini is one of the most versatile; it can be eaten raw, pickled, sautéed, grilled, roasted and even baked into delicious breads and muffins. This mild summer squash adapts well to different recipes because it absorbs flavor exceptionally well. When eaten raw, it's refreshing and crunchy, while roasting brings out its inner sweetness and grilling gives it a smoky flavor.

1. Like avocados, tomatoes, peppers and squash, zucchinis aren't really a vegetable at all. While they're known to be absolutely delicious in savory dishes, they have seeds which run through their core, making them a fruit by definition.

2. The most common variety of zucchini available are deep green in color, but there are many others to choose from. Whether it's pale green, striped, yellow or orange, whichever you find at the farmers market or grocery store, try it out they can all be used interchangeably in recipes.

3. Outside of North America, you'll often find zucchinis labelled as the French word courgettes, squash or summer

squash. But don't be fooled by the name, as they're the same varieties that are grown closer to home.

4. Usually at the beginning of the growing season, you can often buy the vibrant yellow, orange and green blossoms from immature zucchinis. These blossoms, or flowers, are edible and have a wonderful, delicate flavor. They can be stuffed with soft cheese and herbs, fried in a light batter, sautéed with butter and sea salt or torn into a summery salad.

5. Try to buy zucchini that is small to medium in size, as the larger ones are more fibrous. This means they will have more seeds, a woodier texture and may be bitterer. However, if you happen to have large ones on hand, they can easily be grated and baked into loaves or muffins, as they'll cook just as well and be balanced out by the sweetness in a batter.

Did you know Canada holds a zucchini world record? The longest zucchini ever recorded was grown in Brampton, Ontario by Gurdial Singh Kanwal. It measured a whopping 7 ft, 10.3 in. Zucchini and other soft-skinned summer squashes are usually pretty easy to grow. But, gardeners do sometimes face struggles with these productive crops.

Perhaps your vines stopped producing in mid-summer? Or the fruits were small or deformed? Or maybe your plants simply died before producing any fruits? If you found yourself asking why zucchini growing problems struck your garden, this solution guide is for you.

TOP ZUCCHINI GROWING PROBLEMS

Here are ten reasons why you may have faced zucchini growing problems in the past, and tips for making sure these issues don't happen again.

1: Improper variety selection.

Not all zucchini varieties perform the same. Some are more productive than others, and some are more disease- and pest-resistant. First and foremost, when selecting zucchini varieties for your garden, be sure to seek out disease and pest resistance whenever possible. Varieties with a high level of natural resistance often perform better and produce longer. 'Tigress', 'Green Machine', 'Burpee Golden Glory', and 'Yellow Fin' are great choices.

2: Squash vine borers.

One of the biggest zucchini growing problems is a pest known as the squash vine borer. Adult vine borers are day-flying moths that are black and red with dark wings. They're fast flyers, so gardeners don't often spot them. The damage caused by their larvae, however, is difficult to miss. Squash vine borer larvae feed inside the main stem of the plant, hollowing it out and eventually causing plant death. You'll see crumbly, sawdust-like waste collected below a small hole at the base of the plant. To prevent squash vine borers, protect the lower portion of the stem with a wrap of aluminum foil (more on this technique here), or cover the plants with floating row cover until they come into bloom to keep the female moths away from egg-laying sites.

3: Poor pollination.

Zucchini and other squash are insect pollinated, meaning a bee, beetle, or other pollinator is needed to move the pollen from a separate male flower over to a female flower. If there aren't enough pollinators present, puny or deformed fruits are the result. If your zucchini are malformed and stubby on the blossom end, poor pollination is the most pressing of your zucchini growing problems. To improve pollination rates, plant lots of flowering herbs and annuals in and around your zucchini patch. You can also hand-pollinate the vines by using a paintbrush or your fingertip to transfer pollen from the male flowers to the females (more on how to hand pollinate here). Another option is to plant a parthenocarpic variety that doesn't require pollination to set fruit, such as 'Easypick Gold', 'Partenon', or 'Cavili'.

4: Powdery mildew.

Powdery mildew is among the most pervasive fungal diseases when it comes to vine crops like zucchini. This pathogen makes the leaves appear to be covered in a talcum powder-like coating. Though it's primarily an aesthetic issue, severe cases can lead to reduced photosynthesis and reduced production. To overcome powdery mildew, space plants properly give each one plenty of room so air can circulate and dry off wet foliage. Plant only resistant varieties, such as 'Anton', 'Dunja',

'Astia', and 'Emerald Delight', to help combat powdery mildew which is one of the most tenacious zucchini growing problems. Organic fungicides based on potassium bicarbonate (such as GreenCure and BiCarb) are effective as preventatives, as are those based on Bacillus subtilis (such as Serenade).

5: Squash bugs.

When it comes to insects that attack squash, none are more difficult to control than squash bugs. These shield-shaped, brown insects suck out plant juices with their needle-like mouthpart, causing stippling, yellowing, and browning of the leaves. Squash bugs are one of the worst zucchini growing problems a gardener can face. Squash bugs are first seen as clusters of bronze, football-shaped eggs followed by gray nymphs that feed in groups.

The best way to manage squash bugs is to head to the garden every day and inspect the top and bottom of your zucchini leaves for clusters of bronze-colored, football-shaped eggs. Squash bugs are resistant to most pesticides, but very young nymphs can be controlled with applications of insecticidal soap or horticultural oil.

6: Poor soil.

Zucchini doesn't require excessively nutrient-rich soil, but it does perform best in soils that are high in organic matter with a soil pH around 6.5. If your pH is too far off that target mark, the plants may fail to produce quality fruit because the soil pH affects the availability of many different nutrients (more on soil pH here). You can also prevent many zucchini growing problems related to the soil by limiting the amount of nitrogen you add to your garden. Excessive nitrogen produces a lot of green leaves, often at the expense of good fruit production. Use only balanced, organic fertilizers on your zucchini patch and test your soil every few years to ensure it's healthy and well-balanced.

7: Lack of water.

Zucchini growing problems can also stem from irregular soil moisture levels. If plants are allowed to dry out between watering, fruit production can be negatively impacted. Drought stress is never good for vegetable crops, and zucchinis require consistent, even soil moisture throughout the growing season. If Mother Nature doesn't supply your garden with at least one inch of water per week, it's your job to add supplemental irrigation to prevent any possible issues. A 2-3 inch thick layer of mulch helps stabilize soil moisture levels and can reduce the need to irrigate during the hot summer months.

8: Blossom end rot.

Zucchini can also be affected by blossom end rot, just like tomatoes and peppers. This physiological disorder causes the blossom end of the fruit to rot into a dark, sunken canker. It's caused by a calcium deficiency, but it's the result of inconsistent watering. Calcium can only come into a plant as it absorbs water in through its roots. When there's no water in the soil to absorb, the plant can't access calcium either and blossom end rot is the result. To prevent blossom end rot from striking your zucchini, make sure the plants receive ample, consistent applications of water throughout the growing season. Adding more calcium will not solve the problem.

9: Bacterial wilt.

Though this pathogen tends to be more problematic on cucumbers, it sometimes strikes zucchini as well. Sadly, this is one of those zucchini growing problems that's the kiss-of-death when it strikes. Spread by the cucumber beetle, bacterial wilt causes otherwise healthy plants to wilt and die without prior warning. To combat potential problems, keep cucumber beetles in check by trapping them on yellow sticky cards fastened to stakes just above the tops of the plants.

10: Not enough sun.

Though it isn't the worst of the zucchini growing problems you might face, lack of sun can definitely affect plant health and production. Zucchini plants need a minimum of six to eight hours of full sun per day. Lower light levels can result in long, lanky plants with pale green foliage and reduced yields. Poor pollination can also be a side effect of light levels that are too low because pollinators tend to prefer foraging in sunnier areas, particularly on cooler days. Select a full-sun site when planting your zucchinis.

HOW TO PLANT ZUCCHINI

When planting zucchini, you can plant them either as individual plants or grouped on hills. How you grow zucchini squash is up to you, based on how many zucchini plants you intend to grow and how much room you have to grow them.

INDIVIDUAL ZUCCHINI PLANTS

After the chance of frost has passed, plant two to three seeds 36 inches (91.5 cm.) apart. The seeds should be planted about an inch (2.5 cm.) deep. Thin to one plant per spot once the seeds have sprouted and have grown their first set of true leaves.

ZUCCHINI PLANTS
ON A HILL

After the chance of frost has passed, mound up soil about 6 – 12 inches high and 12 – 24 inches (30.5 to 61 cm.) wide. On the top of the hill, in a circle, plant four or five zucchini seeds. Thin the seedlings down to two or three per hill once the seedlings have their first set of true leaves. You can also start zucchini indoors in order to get a head start on the season. Start zucchini seeds indoors four to six weeks before the last frost date and plant them out in the garden after all chances of frost have passed.

INFORMATION ON GROWING ZUCCHINI

Once seedlings are established, mulch around the plants. Mulching helps to keep the ground temperature stable and also helps the soil retain water. These two things will help the zucchini plant have an earlier and larger crop. Make sure that your zucchini plants get at least 2 inches (5 cm.) of water a week. If you don't receive enough rainfall, supplement with manual watering. Use a soaker hose or another method to water the plants below their leaves as watering using a sprinkler can cause the zucchini plants to develop powdery mildew. Harvest zucchini squash when the fruits are small. This will result in a tenderer and flavorful squash.

CONCLUSION

In some cultures, the zucchini flower is considered a delicacy. You can either deep-fry it or sprinkle it raw atop salads, soups, and stews. Zucchini can be eaten raw or cooked in soups, stews, sandwiches, salads, baked goods, and more.

Zucchini is a versatile squash rich in vitamins, minerals, and plant compounds. It may offer several health benefits, ranging from improved digestion to a lower risk of heart disease. Zucchini may aid your bones, thyroid, and prostate. If you're curious, try adding this soft, mild fruit to your diet today.

9 798681 587385